COPYRIGHT

CONTENTS

CHAPTER ONE

Introduction

My thinking sucked. I don't know what else to say about it. I spent most of my life living in silent dread of the unknown future. I worried a lot. I got angry a lot. I was impatient, moody, and irritable. Even when things were going well for me, I worried. In fact, sometimes it seemed like the better my life got, the more afraid I became. With every success or accomplishment came new fears and worries. I imagined things to be happening that weren't. I imagined people to be thinking about me who didn't. I was suffering silently, getting beat up by my own mind.

I eventually got tired of it. I was tired of being afraid. I was tired of souring relationships with my anxiety. I was tired of worrying about things that never happened. I wanted to be happy and free. I began reading everything I could about overcoming anxiety, fear, and worry. I talked to people about it. I went to lectures and listened to podcasts and watched videos. I went to therapy. I went to AA. I went to Yoga and I learned to meditate. I learned everything I could about how to overcome negative thinking from anyone who knew or claimed to know anything about it.

My life became a kind of experiment. I decided I would test the things I learned for myself. I gave everything I learned a fair shot, seeing what worked and what didn't. What I can tell you is there is a lot of garbage out there. I have tried all kinds of tactics. I have tried behavioral modification. I have tried only thinking positive thoughts. I have tried to ignore my thinking. I have tried being grateful that I am not as bad off as the next person. I have tried to "play the tape through" and forecast what the outcomes of my actions might be. Most of these were just a waste of time.

I wrote this book to share with you the best of what I learned. Everything you find in the pages that follow are techniques that have worked for me and continue to work for me. Until the mind is trained, it needs to be monitored all the time. This book will help you understand how the mind works, how to monitor what it's doing, and how to correct it when it starts getting into mischief. I hope you find these suggestions useful. I hope they help you on your own journey to overcome negative thinking. You don't have to spend the rest of your life in fear and worry. You can go from being miserable and afraid to being full of joy and freedom. I have, and you can too!

CHAPTER TWO

Your Mind is Trying to Kill You

Place one hand over one ear and one hand over the other ear and repeat after me:

I have found the enemy and I've got him trapped!

- A Quote from my friend Rob

Have you ever felt like your brain is trying to kill you? I have. My best thinking HAS nearly gotten me killed a few times. It ruined a lot of opportunities. It caused me a lot of anxiety. It caused me to lapse into depressive states that lasted weeks or months. My very best thinking caused me trouble in my relationships at work, with my family, with my neighbors, and often even with strangers. My thinking was never my friend. My brain was always out to get me.

The good news is I don't like pain and suffering. I got tired of my life and began searching for an answer.

After a lot of effort I have isolated THE problem:

My mind is the problem!

That's right. The mind is the problem. Every difficulty you are having today is the result of the thought patterns of your mind. Some people say your actions are the problem and changing them is the answer. To that I say: actions are a symptom. A result. An outcome. Although your actions ultimately create or destroy your life, actions don't happen on their own. Actions are the end result of repetitive thoughts. If there were no thoughts, there would be no actions. Actions are the end of the pattern, not the beginning.

Your actions originate from repetitive thought patterns in the mind. Even as you read this, your mind is generating thoughts that will eventually turn into actions; and for the most part, it is doing this unwatched, unattended, and unregulated. This concept is crucial for you to understand. You need to know exactly what the problem is and how it operates if you are going to fix it.

People who try to change their actions without changing their thinking eventually end up right back where they started. Trying to alter your behavior, your actions, is hacking at the leaves of the problem. You need to get to the root of the problem to make a change that lasts. The root of every problem you have resides in the repetitive thoughts you think every day.

Change your thinking, and your actions will naturally change on their own.

The question becomes, how exactly do you alter your thought patterns? That's exactly what I intend to show you how to do. If you can change your thinking, you will change your life. The rest of this book is going to help you understand where thoughts come from, how to monitor them, and how to alter them as they happen. So read on!

CHAPTER THREE

You Do Not Generate Your Thoughts

Here is the first thing you need to know to change your thinking: most of the time, you do not generate your own thoughts. Unfortunately, most people think they ARE generating their thoughts, or worse, that they are their thoughts. They think if a thought is coming into their consciousness, then it must be coming from their consciousness. This is incorrect. You don't have to take my word for it, just ask yourself this question:

If you were, in fact, in control of generating your thoughts, would you ever deliberately choose a negative one?

Really think about that question. If you were in charge of your thinking, why would you ever choose a negative thought? Would you ever choose a fearful thought on purpose? Would you ever choose a hateful thought? A racist thought? A violent thought? You wouldn't. If you were in control of your thinking, if you were honestly in charge of what you got to think about, you would NEVER deliberately think a negative thought. So if you would never deliberately CHOOSE negative thoughts, and you have them anyway, then you are not always in charge of your thinking.

Have you ever been going through the motions of your day and all of the sudden noticed what you were thinking about and felt bad for having that thought in your head? I have. Have you ever wondered where in the world "that" thought came from? Of course you have. We all have. The mind acts like a computer with no pop up blocker. Thoughts just pop up in your consciousness without warning and without invitation. We are definitely not generating most of our thoughts.

This is important to understand. I want you to PROVE to yourself that you are not always in control of your thinking. Here's how: Please do the following experiment. It takes exactly one minute and will be very eye opening for you:

1. Set your timer on your phone or clock alarm for one minute.
2. For one minute try as HARD as you can to NOT have any thoughts.
3. Count how many thoughts you have in one minute.

Go ahead, do this now.

How'd that go? If you are like most people, you probably had anywhere from 20 - 35 thoughts. If you were paying attention, you might have also noticed that when you have one thought, you have five to ten more thoughts join in before you are able to cease thinking again. So, we can draw a couple conclusions about your thinking from this experiment:

One: Even trying as hard as you can, you CANNOT stop your thoughts from coming. Therefor, you are not in control of many of the thoughts you have. Even if you don't want them, they still come.

Two: Thoughts attract more thoughts, like magnets. One thought pulls five to ten more thoughts to itself.

Pretty scary isn't it? Your mind is thinking ALL the time without your permission and without your control. The good news is, we are not completely incapable of controlling our thinking. If we didn't have the ability to control some of our thinking we'd be totally screwed. We would be puppets on a string controlled by the mind. We do have "some" choice in what we think.

Try this experiment too. Choose right now to think a happy thought. Imagine a time when you were really happy, and bring it into full consciousness. Recall the sounds and sights and smells of that moment. Recall how you felt. You can probably relive the event entirely.

So we can say from this experiment that you do have the ability to seize control of your thoughts and decide what you want to think about! This is another really important concept to understand. Some thoughts are going to come at us whether we want them to or not.

They are almost impossible to stop, even if we try with all our effort. But, we do get to choose some of the thoughts we think, and have full conscious control over them.

This is good news. Without the ability to choose at least some of your thoughts, what do you think your mind would think about most of the time? I don't know about you, but my mind rarely thinks of anything positive on its own. I don't know why but my mind naturally thinks negative thoughts of worry, self-pity, jealousy, anger, fear, endless desires, past hurts, future concerns, schemes of every kind. It worries about money, property, prestige, and what other people are doing. It judges other people. It wallows in self-pity. It baffles me. It embarrasses me and I don't like it. But because we have the power to choose at least some of our thoughts, we have the power to override a lot of the garbage the mind throws at us all time.

Just to recap because this is so important:

#1: We do not generate many of our thoughts.

#2: We can't stop those thoughts from coming even when we try really hard.

#3: Thoughts are magnetic and attract other thoughts.

#4: We do have the ability to choose some of our thoughts.

These are critical concepts you need to understand about your mind and your thinking. For me, these concepts were the keys to the gateway of freedom. Once I became aware that I was not always in charge of my thoughts, but had the ability to control some of them, I realized I really needed to start paying attention to what my mind was doing. My brain was bombarding me constantly with negativity and I wasn't doing anything to change it. I have learned how to use the power to choose my thoughts to conquer negative thinking, and I am going to show you exactly how I did it.

CHAPTER FOUR

First Notice That You Are Thinking

The first thing you have to do to change your thoughts is to start paying attention to them. If you are like most people, your mind is like a child that has been allowed to do whatever it wants for a very long time. And just like a child, a mind that has never been monitored has no boundaries and has gotten very used to being unruly. But now, maybe for the first time, you are going to start paying attention to what that child doing. This is the first step in the process.

It is going to take some practice. Very few of us have been trained to do this. Most of the time you are completely detached from what your mind is doing up there. But starting today you are going to begin noticing what thoughts are coming through. Simply begin checking in with yourself as often as you can, just to see what you are thinking about at that moment. This is how you begin.

How often do you need to monitor your thoughts? Initially, you need to monitor them as often as you can. Remember, your mind is never NOT thinking, and if you aren't in control of what it's thinking about, it's probably thinking about nonsense.

If your mind really was a three year old child, how often would you check in to see what your three year old is doing? This practice is just like that. It doesn't take any time at all for a child to get itself into mischief. Your mind is the same. If you are not monitoring your thoughts, you won't even notice anything is wrong until your mind ruins your day. If you are going to become a master of conquering negative thinking, it is absolutely critical that you monitor your thoughts as often as you can.

At first, if you notice your thought patterns even a few times a day, that's great. Again, you haven't been trained to pay attention to what your mind is doing all the time. It's going to take some practice to get in the habit. The ultimate goal is to pay attention to what you are thinking every moment of the day. But for now, just start where you are and do the best you can. Even if you only check in with your thoughts once per day, that's probably a 100% improvement over the day before. It doesn't matter how you start, but start today.

Here are some suggestions for getting started

One way to get started is to pick an event that happens periodically throughout every day of your life; agree that each time that event happens you will check in and see what your mind is doing. For you, it might be every time you walk the dog, or check your e-mail, or log into Facebook. You might even set a chime on your phone to go off periodically throughout your day just as a reminder to check in with your thinking. Pick an event, and use that as a trigger to remind you to check in with your thoughts.

You can also place notes in your path. You can put notes on the fridge, on the dashboard of your car, on your desk, on your computer's screen saver; get a custom coffee mug made that says, "What are you thinking about?" Do whatever you need to do to remind yourself to check in every so often and see what your mind is doing.

You can also determine what type of thought patterns you are thinking by your mood. Why? Because thought patterns generate moods. If you are feeling bad, chances are you've been thinking negative thoughts. Be aware of your moods. They will reveal what you've been thinking about. Moods are also a great reminder about the importance of monitoring your thoughts. Unless you like being in a bad mood all the time - and I assume if you are reading this book you don't - it is CRITICAL that you monitor your thought patterns as often as you can. Your moods will always tell on your mind.

Another great tool is to keep a journal or your positive and negative thoughts as they come up. Divide a page in half lengthwise and at the top of one side write "positive" and on the other half write "negative." Whenever you notice you have a negative thought, put a check mark on that side. Whenever you notice you have a positive thought, put a check mark on the other side. Review this at the end of the day (without judgment) and see how you did.

This is a very old practice. Sages of old would keep a bag of white marbles and a bag of black marbles. When they had a negative thought, they moved a black marble to the opposite bag. When they had a positive thought, they would move a white marble. They counted them up at the end of the day and did it again the next day. This is how they kept track of their thinking. Today we call this practice: Mindfulness

What I can tell you from experience is, if you practice paying attention to your thought patterns every day, pretty soon you get really good at living your life. Negative thoughts rarely get by me unnoticed. I don't always take care of them as fast as I should, but when negative thoughts crop up (and they do) I hear them and employ any one of the tactics you are about to learn to overcome them. If they can't gain momentum, they can't wreck my day.

Work hard to become a student of your own mind. Pay attention to what you are thinking.

CHAPTER FIVE

Next Try To Arrest That Thought

Now that you are paying attention to what your mind is doing, let's get down to dealing with the thoughts that come. You ARE going to have negative thoughts. That's just the way it is. I do believe it is possible to completely eliminate all negative thoughts, but I think it takes a lifetime of practice. For the rest of us mortals, let's just assume that you will have to contend with negative thinking. After all - life happens!

Often negative thinking gets triggered by an event; something happens. Maybe you made a mistake at your office, or you just found out a friend is sick. You have a flat tire, woke up late for work, got a crappy e-mail, or something like that. This is the hardest type of negative thinking to overcome because it comes at us so fast. You might find yourself in the middle of dealing with the details of the event while simultaneously trying to stop a negative thought-train before it gets rolling.

Here's an example of an event that happened to me in the past:

The company I worked for was relocating me to a different state. I was really looking forward to it. The movers were supposed to arrive on a Saturday morning and pack up the U-Haul and we were going to leave later that night.

Then, two weeks before I was due to move, the vice-president of the company informed me that I had to travel with him for "training" the ENTIRE week before we moved. I was going to have to leave on Monday morning, and be gone all week, and not return until late Friday night, which was the night before the movers were coming. The Vice President knew I was moving and when. It felt like they were doing this on purpose just to screw with me; something they were known for doing. I e-mailed them to remind them that I was moving and asked if we could do the training after I moved. They said no.

Once I realized there was no way out of this, my thought pattern was:

My wife is going to be SO pissed. I'm not even going to be home to help her prepare. She's going to have to do everything alone. I won't have time to say goodbye to our friends! Those assholes! They know I have to move and they know this is the week I have to prepare for it. This training is bullshit and could be done any time. They are doing this on purpose! Oh my god - my

17

wife is going to be so pissed off at me. How can they do this to me? I'd quit right now if I could! Maybe I should quit. Screw them!

I went from being in a good mood and looking forward to the future in one moment to being furious and ready to quit and trash my future the next. I got some bad news and BAM - my mind races off into the future, full of fear and anger.

This was my typical response to everything. Maybe your response is to shut down, go into denial, punish, control, become passive-aggressive, or any number of other unproductive behaviors. This is the kind of thinking you need to learn how to stop if you are going to be happy and peaceful. You can't stop life from happening. What you have to learn is how to control your reactions to it. You have to learn how to interrupt these old negative thought patterns before they gain momentum and if they do get going, you need to know how to stop them. That's what the rest of this book is about.

Here's the first way to try and stop them:

Slam on the brakes!

When you get some bad news or something happens, and you hear the negative thought train rolling out, hit the brakes as hard as you can. Make every effort to catch that thought before it goes anywhere. You know what your pattern is, and you know what the outcome will be: negative emotions and then on to negative actions. So as soon as something happens in your life, try with all your will power to stop your thinking before it can gain momentum.

This is how I do it:

"Yes, this is unfair. I don't like it. But I have been through difficult times before, and I have gotten through them. Ten years from now I probably won't even remember this. I just need to focus on positivity and do what I can to reduce the unpleasantness, and as best I can, maintain my peace of mind. It probably won't be as bad as I think. It never is! Who knows, this might be a blessing in disguise. Things that seem unpleasant at first often are. Maybe it will be o.k. let's just see what happens."

It's critical for you to develop your own method for arresting the negative thought train before it gets very far. If you don't, all kinds of things can happen. Maybe you over-react and quit a job before you have a new job (I have). Maybe you get in a big fight with your spouse and feelings of bitterness settle into your relationship. Maybe you let resentment settle in for the people who caused the event and it destroys the relationship (lots of business partnerships have ended this way). All of these things have happened to me before.

But even if nothing catastrophic happens, it will still be costly. When you get angry or upset, your creativity disappears. Your ability to problem-solve evaporates. You make mistakes. You forget little details, which causes more frustration. You lose the enjoyment of the moment, and things that should have been pleasant and enjoyable become an exercise in frustration and anger. You will probably make everyone around you miserable. All of this happens if you don't stop negative thoughts when they come up. You pay a HUGE price for not learning how to stop all of this from happening.

Think of it like an avalanche: If you start a rock teetering at the top of the mountain and you catch it soon enough, its very easy to stop. But once it starts tumbling down, it's a lot harder to catch. Once it gains momentum and other rocks start rolling too, it's impossible to stop and all you can do is watch the disaster happen. Negative thinking is just like that. So stop that rock from rolling immediately!

It will take a lot of practice before you will be able to do this all the time. In fact, if you can do this just "some" of the time, you are well on your way to controlling stinking thinking. Me? I'm probably successful at this about half the time. So don't worry if you try and do not succeed right away. Just try the best you can to improve from maybe 5% success to 30% success. Don't beat yourself up. Just work toward improvement until it becomes habit. This is just one way to stop negative thinking once it starts. Keep reading. I am going to arm you with many more tools. When one doesn't work, try another!

CHAPTER SIX

Think Opposite Thoughts

There are going to be a lot of times when you fail to stop the negative thought-train from leaving the station. That's o.k. Just expect it. It happens. I can't tell you how many times this has happened to me. Something irritates or frightens me, I hear my first negative thought loud and clear, I try with all my might to focus on not letting it go forward, and it goes forward anyway. Like I said, I probably succeed in stopping it about half the time. The good news is, even rolling full steam ahead, you can still stop it.

If you fail to stop negative thoughts when they start, stop them as fast as you can.

Try this next:

When negative thoughts come - think the opposite thought.

I learned this originally in AA. People would say: whatever your first thought is - do the opposite. They said to take opposite actions and to think opposite thoughts.

Long before AA, (a few thousand years before) a guy named Patanjali wrote the Yoga Sutras. The entire process he outlined was designed to conquer the troubles of the mind. He suggested:

When negative thoughts come - think their opposite.

Here is an example of how to use this:

Let's say you are driving to work and someone is tailgating you. You look back in your rear view mirror, and they are weaving back and forth, two feet from your bumper. They keep speeding up and slowing down, getting closer each time. You can almost feel their anger. As this is happening, you think: You stupid asshole!
If you are paying attention to your thinking, you will notice what you've just thought. As fast as you can, think the opposite thought. Maybe something like this:

No, he's not a jerk. Maybe he's late for work and scared of losing his job. I've been there before. I know how awful it feels to be late. I will let him pass when I can. I hope he is o.k.

Here's another example. This is a pretty common thought:

Good grief, I have to go to work today

Think the opposite thought: I GET to go to work today. I chose this job. Lots of people are unemployed. It may not perfect, but it supports me for now. I might change it some day, but for now I am grateful to have employment that pays my bills.

Try a few on your own. Think the opposite thought:

My boss is such a bitch!
He is such a loud-mouthed jerk!
I have to get this sale!
I'm fat.
I never do anything right.
My life sucks.
Other people suck.

If you are like me, on any given day you've probably had every one of these thoughts. And each one of these thoughts has attracted a host of friends, and they've had a negativity party in your head. It is so important to hear these thoughts as you think them, and to immediately supplant that negative thought with its opposite. I do this a lot and it helps me regain perspective.

Some readers might find this a little "fluffy." But is it? Thinking opposite thoughts isn't about kidding yourself into feeling better. It isn't that. It is simply acknowledging that our minds complain a lot, think the worst a lot, and are often either partially or completely wrong. Thinking opposite thoughts simply brings things into perspective.

Just to recap so far: Pay attention to your thinking. Try to stop negative thoughts as soon as they start. If you can't, go right to compelling your mind to think opposite thoughts!

CHAPTER SEVEN

Ask Yourself If This Thought Is True

The next tactic you can employ to end negative thinking is to start inspecting your thinking for accuracy. Ask yourself how many of your negative thoughts are accurate? Are they factual? Can gather plenty of hard evidence to support the validity of your thoughts? I don't know about you, but most of my negative thoughts are simply not true. When I hear a negative thought come, I ask myself:

Is that true? Is it accurate?

Usually it is not. Discovering for myself that a negative thought is wrong, or unsubstantiated, is one of the easiest ways I have found to quiet a negative thought. If it isn't true, then why continue believing it? Why let it bother you?

Here's a great way to begin the practice of inspecting your thoughts for accuracy so you can dispel them. Start by examining any thought you have that include the words always or never. Thoughts that include these words are almost always inaccurate, and yet, they are some of the most common thoughts have.

They sound like this:

She **always** does that to me!
He is **always** late!
I **always** get the bad end of the deal!
I **never** get what I want!
Traffic in that part of town is **always** bad!
American Airlines is **never** on time!
My Mom **always** does this to me!
My boss **never** takes any of my suggestions!
She **never** listens to me!

If a thought includes the word always or never, it's wrong. Why? Because nothing is ALWAYS one-way or NEVER another way. So any time you hear a thought about yourself or others that includes always or never, it's wrong. Nobody always does anything, and neither do you. The word never is a self-pity party starter. When you speak or think in absolutes, you are being inaccurate. When you hear thoughts taking an absolute form like always and never, it's an exaggeration, which is a five-syllable word for LIE!

Whenever you hear yourself saying or thinking that you (or they) always do something, stop yourself and remember this:

Nobody always does anything. This thought is inaccurate, and it is counter-productive.

These thoughts are some of the most insidious thoughts in our minds because they are so common. We hear them and use them without being mindful of what we are saying or thinking. We have to begin paying attention to these kinds of thoughts. They are a destructive pattern of thinking that has NO upside for you.

As you attempt to practice doing this technique, you'll hear your brain say something like, "O.k., they don't always do it, but they do it a lot!" This is most likely inaccurate as well. Obscure thoughts like "often" are usually exaggerated. But if your mind is stubborn (like my mind is) and insists that something does happen a lot or often, then say to yourself: Let's assign an EXACT number to this vague claim of often. How many times (exactly) has this happened recently? Give me an exact count!

How many times in the last year (or ten years) have you not gotten your way? Bad things happen to you often? How often? How many times exactly? Make your mind assign a number to it. If you are capable of being honest with yourself, it probably isn't all that often after all. Your mind is just trying to throw a pity party for itself, so it says, "Things usually don't work out for me." Don't give in to this vague claim of the mind. Insist it provide data or be quiet.

Our minds are so busy churning out false information, it's a wonder we ever have a good day. Today I operate under the assumption that most of what I believe to be true is based on partial information (at best) about what happened. Therefor, what I believe to be true, is probably incorrect, or at best, only partially correct. With this in mind, I don't take my thoughts so seriously. Most of them are wrong, or, at best, mostly wrong.

You can do this with your whole life story and probably make yourself feel a lot better about it. Go back and examine every story you have been telling yourself about how you were treated, who has hurt you, and how you let yourself or others down. Really go back and examine JUST THE FACTS of the event. Drop the story about how it made you feel and the events that followed. Just look at the facts of the event and nothing else. Would everyone else draw the exact same conclusions you have? Would everyone else see it like you do? Maybe not. Maybe you don't remember it right at all. And again, if a thought (story) isn't accurate, why keep dragging it around?

Over time, you can get really good at this. Inaccurate thinking IS negative thinking. It is a pattern of the mind that has settled in and gone unexamined. Think of a negative thought pattern like a deep groove you've carved into your consciousness. By interrupting the thought pattern and examining thoughts for accuracy, you discover many of your thoughts are wrong. You can replace those thoughts with accurate thoughts that serve you. Over time you can start to wear that groove down. If you practice long enough, maybe you will eliminate the old pattern and carve a new, more positive pattern of thinking. If the only thing you ever accomplished was eliminating all inaccurate thoughts from your mind, you will have come a long way toward happiness and peace of mind.

So just to recap: Learn to pay attention to your thought. When negative thoughts come, and you can't stop them in their tracks, or you struggle to think their opposite, go right to asking yourself if the thought is accurate. Chances are, it isn't. And if a thought isn't accurate, it isn't worth carrying around any longer.

CHAPTER EIGHT

What's The Worst That Can Happen

At this point you are probably saying to yourself:

Yeah but some of my worries are legitimate!

Great! You've discovered that a few of your negative thoughts have validity. It happens. For example, if your car breaks down, the rent is due tomorrow, you have $1,000 in the bank, and it is going to cost $1,000 to fix the car, it IS going to cause you REAL, financial discomfort. The rent is still due.

However, even when you know for sure that you are going to face some kind of struggle, it's still important, maybe more important than any other time, to control your fear, worry, and doubt. Don't take an event that is going to suck regardless of what you do, and make it 10,000 times worse with your mind. Here's what I do when something happens and I know for sure discomfort is on the way. I ask myself this question:

What's the worst case scenario? What's the worst that COULD happen?

My mind is really good at the worst case scenario game. So I totally let it run wild with worst case scenarios (which is what it wants to do anyway). As an example, let's say I totally screw up in my business, and I lose a customer because of it. It's a big account and it is going to cost me a lot of money in lost sales. These are the facts.

I let my mind run with what it thinks the worst case scenario could be:

I could go bankrupt and not be able to pay my bills. My credit might be ruined. I could lose my business and my home. I would be totally embarrassed in front of my friends and family. My girlfriend might leave me. I might end up homeless and penniless and have to relocate. I may not be able to get a good job if my credit is ruined. I might end up poor the rest of my life because of this!

So now I've got the worst case scenario. I've got it right there in front of me. Next I say to myself:

Fine. Let's say that the worst case scenario DOES happen:

If every single one of these things happens, can I handle it? (Usually I can)

What is the likelihood that the worst case scenario WILL happen? (Pretty unlikely)

Have I been in worse situations than this and gotten through it? (Usually)

Have I ever exaggerated a problem in my mind that never happened? (Often)

How often have I thought something was a total disaster and it turned out to be the best thing that could have happened? (Usually)

Is there any action I can take right now to impact the situation to make sure the worst case scenario does not happen? (If yes - write down what that is)

Am I going to be o.k. no matter what? (Yep)

It helps me a lot to go through this exercise when I am really freaked out. Whatever I imagine the worse case scenario to be, I have found:

#1: It rarely ever happens.

#2: I've probably been through something similar before or know someone else who has and it came out o.k.

#3: Chances are, there is A LOT I can do to make sure the worst case scenario doesn't happen. Whatever that is, I write it out, get direction, and work toward my own salvation.

#4: No matter what happens - no matter how bad it might be - eventually the dust will settle, and I will move on. No matter what, I will be o.k. (And so will you)

#5: Some day in the future I will probably look at what happened and realize that it was the best thing that ever happened to me, or maybe I learned a lesson I would need later on in life.

To say that everything you worry about is untrue would be inaccurate. Life happens. It's hard to lose a job, or a loved one, or become ill, or have a business fail, or have the car break down when you don't have money. These things suck and create a lot of negative thinking. The key is, even in the worst circumstances, be able to know your worst case scenario, and find a way to look at it calmly.

By imagining your worst case scenario and then breaking it down into manageable questions, you calm the mind. You make the problem appear smaller and the brain quiets down. When the mind becomes quiet and calm, creativity returns, problem solving faculty functions properly, and the mind and body do not fatigue as quickly. This gives you the energy you need to work toward a solution. Trying to tackle a problem before you have calmed your mind is a complete waste of time and often creates more problems than existed originally.

So when panic strikes because something happened, or you think something is going to happen, just start asking yourself what the worst case scenario could be. Ask yourself if it's likely to happen. Think it through and write out what you can do to make sure it doesn't happen. And even if it does, no matter what, over time the dust will settle, and you will adjust. This is life. It isn't always fun. But you can get through it. You always have, and one way or another, you always will.

CHAPTER NINE

Move Your Body

One night, a LONG time ago I was sitting inside my grandparent's house stewing on some negative bullshit. I was full of anxiety. I had tried everything; I thought through the worst case scenario; I asked myself if it was true, and no matter what I tried, I just had this terrible feeling of dread. I couldn't get out of it. It was late at night, so there wasn't really anything to do. When I couldn't take the anxiety any longer, I stood up, put on my shoes, walked outside and kept walking. I walked and walked and walked. I probably walked five miles, which was a big deal for me at the time. I walked around town and out into the countryside. And you know what? I felt better. My mind felt clear, and my sense of dread had gone away. I walked home and slept like a baby. I've been walking ever since then, when I need to clear my mind.

I still practice this today. When I feel tempers heating up at home or hear my crazy mind going, I ask if I can take a moment to gather myself, and I go for a walk. When I come back I am much calmer and can communicate better. I have found little else that works as well for me. Moving the body has NO drawbacks. No harmful effects. So next time you catch yourself stuck in your head, get up, put some shoes on your feet, and go for a walk.

Moving my body is still one of the most successful methods I have ever found for defeating negative thoughts. Here's how I do it:

I go outside and go for a walk. I keep walking until I feel better and rational thinking returns.

That's it. Go outside and go for a walk. You will be amazed at how much you can reduce anxiety this way. I say go outside because there is also something therapeutic about going outside and walking in nature. It is the best. Don't worry about speed or heart rate or distance or any of that. Just go outside and walk until you feel better. Keep it simple.

But let's say you can't go outside. Maybe you are at work in an office and your boss is a total jerk and there is NO WAY for you to go outside. No problem - here are some alternatives to walking outdoors:

- Sixty seconds of jumping jacks - repeat three times
- Stairs - find a flight of stairs and walk up and down it until you start to feel better

- Go down to the parking garage and walk up a few flights of parking deck
- Go up to the roof and walk around in squares until you feel better

You are not into walking? That's o.k. Do whatever works for you. I have also gone to the driving range and hit golf balls. I like to run. I used to ride bikes on trails. You could go bowling. Hit the gym. Go to a Yoga class or take one online. Hit a punching bag. I don't really care what you do. But when the negative thought train has left the station, move the body, and you will almost instantly feel better. I like walking because it doesn't require any prep work, and there is no time delay (you don't have to drive to the driving range angry), and you don't need anything special to do it. But do what works for you.

Try this. Next time you notice you've gotten in a funk, move your body until you feel better. Who cares if it costs you 20 minutes? Your bad mood will cost you far more.

CHAPTER TEN

Focus On What Your Are Doing

If there is some reason you cannot get up and move your body, this is the next thing you should try:

Get FULLY engaged in what you are doing right now.

I had the opportunity to work with a spiritual advisor who was a master at not letting negativity ruin the day. I would call him when I got upset, and he would help me get out of it. He would say to me, "Is there anything wrong right now?"

I would say, "Yes, I'm so angry I can't even think straight!"

To that he would say, "Yes, but right now, this moment, is there anything actually wrong? Has anything actually changed since right before you got angry?"

I would hesitate, think, and say, "No, just this second, nothing has actually changed."

He would say, "Then the only thing that has changed is that you are thinking about what is bothering you. Go back to work, and focus on what needs to be done today. You are in sales, do you need to make sales calls today?"

I would say, "Yes, I do, but I can't right now. I'm too upset."

He would say, "No, you are not. Yes, you can make sales calls, and you need to. Unless you want to be upset AND have less money next week, your job today is to make sales calls. So for now, forget about this problem, go sit at your desk, and make your sales calls. And if this is still a crisis later tonight, you call me back, and we'll talk more."

And I would. I would go back to my desk reluctantly, pick up my phone and make one call and then another and then another. After twenty minutes or so I would feel fine again and continue on with my day. I rarely had to call him back later. Once my mind was diverted from being upset and refocused on the task at hand, I felt better and my mind calmed down.

This has been an important tactic for me. Getting some bad news or having someone at work piss me off - used to wreck my entire day, and often an entire week. It was particularly problematic for me when I owned my own business because I didn't have a boss. I would convince myself that I couldn't work being so upset. I would lose entire weeks of time waiting for "the right time" when I could do my job. As you can imagine, my business didn't go too well. My mind sabotaged a lot of my days, which ruined opportunities for achieving long-term goals that were important to me.

So when you get upset, refocus and get into what you need to do for that day. It doesn't matter if it is typing an e-mail, answering the phone, reading a book, driving to the office, or riding in a car with a family member - when stinking thinking kicks in and you can't move your body - FORCE your mind to focus on what you are doing right now.

This isn't always easy. When you try to make your mind drop what it's brooding on and demand it focus on the task at hand, it will resist you. It will say things like, "I can't go to work in this condition. I should call in sick." It tells us it's unreasonable to expect to function at a "time like this" and tries to get us to agree to being stuck in a funk all day. But if you persist in focusing and re-focusing, eventually your mind will relent and stop trying to drag you down. It requires effort, but after a few minutes, your mind will usually relent. You just have to keep at it until it does.

Focus on where you are and what you are doing; and exclude all other thoughts. And when they drift back (and they will), say to yourself: "No, you are not going to ruin my day or this moment. I am where I am right now, doing what I am doing right now, and this is what I am focusing on right now." It will take you a few minutes, and your mind will resist, but persist. Before long you won't even remember what was bothering you.

CHAPTER ELEVEN
Sing - REALLY LOUD!

I almost left this chapter out because I thought nobody would actually do it, but it is too powerful to leave out. Singing is a bad-mood buster. I don't care if you can't sing or hate the sound of your own voice; sing anyway, and sing LOUD! If you are in your car, people at the stoplight might laugh at you, but so what. Do you know them? No, so who cares? Do you want to feel better and conquer negative thinking, or do you want to impress strangers you'll never see again? Stopping a bad mood is important business and singing really loud is a great way to do it. So who cares who might be listening - sing anyway. It works!

It doesn't matter what you sing. It really doesn't. I have a few songs I like and I sing them over and over. Even the sound OM repeated over and over again will end a bad mood. So don't worry too much about what you are singing. Just sing as loud as you can, and keep going until you feel yourself relax.

Music is powerful medicine and it's easy. You just have to let go of your ego. It isn't about sounding good. It's about relieving negativity from the mind. Try it! If you don't know any songs, turn on the radio, find a song you know the words to and sing along at the top of your lungs. Again, it doesn't matter how you sound - it only matters that you sing.

Give this a try - it works!

CHAPTER TWELVE

Help Someone Else

This is one of the most difficult things to do, but it is SO powerful. If you are caught in a storm of negative thinking and you turn your attention to someone else and the struggle they are going through, you will temporarily forget about yours. I can't say enough about this. All you have to do is call someone and ask how she is doing and don't share ANY of your current problems or drama. None of it. If you do, you won't listen to her. You'll just be waiting for your turn to talk. Instead, listen. See if you can help them with their troubles. Don't worry if you don't have good guidance for them; most people just need to be heard.

So call somebody. It doesn't matter who. Every person on this planet is suffering. All of them. Just choose anyone in your contacts, dial their number, and ask how they are doing. Give them your full and complete attention. Everybody was born with a deep desire to be listened to; to be heard; to be understood.

Be that person for them. You will be amazed at how good you feel and how small your worries have become by the time you get off the phone.

One of my spiritual advisors made me do this over and over again. His answer to problems was always to call other people and see how they were doing.

He said: You Get Out of Yourself - By Getting Into Others!

He would say, "Call these couple guys and see how they are doing. Get out of yourself. You'll feel better. And when you are done calling them, call me back, and we'll talk about it if you'd like." I never wanted to, but I would call other people and ask how they were doing, and I always felt better. In fact, I rarely needed to call him back. I would be too busy thinking about the person I had just talked to and what they were going through. The fastest way to get out of yourself, is to get into others. Do this. You will be amazed how quickly helping someone else, will calm your own inner storm.

We spend so much time thinking and obsessing about ourselves, it's no wonder we end up in a bad mood. Selfishness is a disease of the mind. Its symptoms are negative thoughts. The fastest way out of selfishness is to behave selflessly; help another human being. It's a prescription for ending negative thoughts, and it is the most powerful way to make sure those thoughts don't start in the first place.

CHAPTER THIRTEEN

Final Thoughts

I hope you have found these suggestions helpful. What you've just read is the best of what I've learned about overcoming negative thoughts. As long as negative thinking dominates your life, you'll end up with negative actions and negative consequences. If people truly understood the role negative thoughts play in shaping their lives, they would make overcoming them their number one priority. I hope you will.

I wanted to share some thoughts with you on how to implement these techniques into your life. You've read through them and have been exposed to the concepts, but putting them into practice is really important. Whenever I learn something new, and I want to implement it, I write the core ideas (like the chapter headings) on my calendar, and I try to practice one concept per day.

I've found this to be really effective. If I only read the materials, I might remember the concepts, but they don't sink in. When I practice one concept per day, however, it stays with me. It's easy to do. Just pick a chapter heading (like Think Opposite Thoughts), put it on your phone calendar, and try to practice that one concept throughout your day. The next day, practice the next one, and so on. This works really well for me.

Most of this book has been about dealing with negative thinking, when it happens. This is a great way to get started. However, if you'd like to learn how to prevent negative thinking from happening in the first place, please watch for my second book on negative thinking, which is all about prevention. You will be able find it online at Amazon.com. Also, if you'd like to e-mail me with questions or concerns, please do so at: tim@timrx.com. Also, you can join my e-mail newsletter for monthly tips on conquering negative thinking and upcoming books at www.timrx.com. I am happy to hear from you and will return all e-mails as quickly as possible.

My main hope is that by reading this book you might reduce negative thinking in your own life. If you've found this material useful, please share it with someone you care about. If reading this book wrecks just one bad mood for them, their world, and the world as a whole will be a little bit better, even if only for a day.

I wish you Love and Light - Tim

ABOUT THE AUTHOR

About The Author

Tim VanDerKamp lives in New Orleans. He teaches yoga, meditation, and how to use mindfulness and the principles contained in this book to live life more fully. He welcomes all inquiries by email at: tim@timrx.com You can join his monthly e-newsletter for more tips on conquering negative thinking by visiting his website at: www.timrx.com

Authors Note: If you've enjoyed this book, please take just one minute of your time to leave a review on the website where you bought the book. You will be doing me a tremendous service. Reviews help self-published authors like me more than you realize.

Sincerely,
Tim

Made in the USA
Middletown, DE
14 September 2018